T0358839

The Widow's Crayon Box

Also by Molly Peacock

Poetry

The Analyst: Poems
The Second Blush
Cornucopia
Original Love
Animals at the Table
Take Heart
Raw Heaven
And Live Apart

Fiction

Alphabetique: 26 Characteristic Fictions

Memoir

Paradise, Piece by Piece

Biography

The Paper Garden: Mrs. Delany Begins Her Life's Work at 72
Flower Diary: Mary Hiester Reid Paints, Travels, Marries &
   Opens a Door

Criticism

How to Read a Poem & Start a Poetry Circle

Play

The Shimmering Verge

Editor

The Private I: Privacy in a Public World (essays)
The Best Canadian Poetry in English

.

The Widow's Crayon Box

POEMS

Molly Peacock

W. W. NORTON & COMPANY

Independent Publishers Since 1923

For information about permission to reproduce selections from this book,
write to Permissions, W. W. Norton & Company, Inc.,
500 Fifth Avenue, New York, NY 10110

For information about special discounts for bulk purchases,
please contact W. W. Norton Special Sales at
specialsales@wwnorton.com or 800-233-4830

Manufacturing by Versa Press
Production manager: Gwen Cullen

ISBN 978-1-324-07943-9

W. W. Norton & Company, Inc., 500 Fifth Avenue, New York, N.Y. 10110
www.wwnorton.com

W. W. Norton & Company Ltd., 15 Carlisle Street, London W1D 3BS

1 2 3 4 5 6 7 8 9 0

In Memory of Michael Groden 1947–2021

Contents

PART ONE: After

PART TWO: Before

The Widow's Crayon Box

PART ONE

After

TOUCHED

When I feel moved and then say I am touched,
it's another presence inside me I sense,
the dip of an oar, a canoe being launched.
I'm the oar, but I'm the water, and sense
at once initiation and response.
After you died, I felt you next to me,
and over months you entered gradually
into that lake and disappeared. Not gone,
but so internalized you're *not* next to me.
You're not the port, or the support; you're done
being you, and my loneliness is so extreme
that I feel moved by almost anything,
even the forehead of a dog that leans
against my knee in an elevator, things
as brief as all the ways you would lean
against me getting a glass of water
at the sink. Everything touches me,
now that I'm not touched, but moved.

THE WIDOW'S CRAYON BOX

1.

A mourning widow is still, gray and mauve.
A mourning widow, umber, barely moves.
She's dun as dread, the green of love removed.
That's what I thought. Then death lit its fire
and anger flared: it was the vermilion
of ~~grief~~ disbelief! When Carolyn called, the ire
of loss ignited—burnt sienna, un-soothed:
She said you appeared on her morning run . . .

Hey, get back here! Help me do our taxes!
(Your mourning widow never relaxes.)

The eight child-colors of crayon boxes
are far too basic and behaved—I feel
the one-fifty-two emotional shades:
a rose one fleurs before a peach one fades.
Scarlet, orchid, cerise umbrellas shield
me from my own tears.
                    Then I yield.

2.

I yield to a turquoise sky, becoming young:
a chartreuse vision of suburban lawns
cut diagonally by a sidewalk, gray,
down which we stroll. Hip to hip. We're sixteen,
loving how our bones meet as we sway
right, left, right, thigh to thigh to lean
against each other all we dare in public,
though on Saturday morning no one's here
on our private plum-green Classics think-walk
after the high school enrichment Plato talk.
Thinking, for us: viridian as sex. Thought-flick!
Same height. Arms around waists. Earlobe. Tongue quick.

Your death face, an abandoned clay quarry
filled with memory water: *I'm sorry, sorry, sorry.*

3.

Often when crying, I say "I'm sorry,"
blue all over again. For why, bluebell-why,
do people beige-say, "I'm sorry to hear that."
I'm stuck in the Sorry Wild Blue Aerie
unable to fledge. *Indigo.* Can't fly.

I wrote down all you said the day you died.
And now can't read it. I'm glad I'm alone.
No one can hear the little yelp-like sighs
pressing involuntarily from my lips.
(Once you passed me, sunk in my poems, and quipped,
"Reading your favorite author?" How we laughed!)

I'm sorry, I'm so sorry, honey. "You've passed,"
is what people say. Sorry = sorrow?
Midnight memory water. I'm alone.

4.

Memory water. Let's swim in it, I say
to my other self. There are two of me,
one to avoid the blue folder, one to say
to my consolers about the other me
that she is practicing self-care—the flare
of heliotrope despair that shoots behind
my wise-old-lady smile as I reassure
the consoler that I've booked a masseur,
have a social worker, and found a kind
yoga instructor, along with friends
planning my birthday, neighbors for a stroll.
They swirl into a palliative scrim. But consolations end.
Let's swim in air—you're air now.

                              I'll drop my dole.

5.

I drop my sorrow like a towel and dive
deep in the manatee water, past algae that,
as I get closer, are floating green running shorts,
running shirts, and, like sea rocks, running shoes.
The water smells of human sweat—yours,
bursting in from a run.

                  Your Death Certificate
is dry—one of the pieces of paper in the blue
folder I avoid. Now I've missed
a Death Benefit deadline. I whine
to our lawyer. "Just scan it and sign,"
she says.

        But everything's moist. A fine mist
saturates the air. Salt tears? Or brine
from marathon oceans of runners' sweat
in the humid climate of being alive.

6.

You're vapor. I'm alive—with no AC!
The three of us—my two young helpers and I
—struggle with humidity till it's fixed.
Each clean shirt we fold emanates a mix
of perspiration, cancer drugs, and mint—
the Dr. Bronner's soap you showered with.
After they fill the giant Ziploc bags,
they leave. And I—

                    unpack the bags!
Getting rid of your clothes? Pure fantasy.
I pluck out thirty-eight pairs of socks and lay
them on the table—stripes and checks, a combo
of Crayola colors: *mango-tango*,
radical red, *purple heart*, and *shadow*,
once paired with Asics, now part of your myth.

7.

Once paired with Asics, now part of your myth,
each sock safety-pinned to its mate.
Stripes and checks forge the Crayola-like smith-
y of your—you *DO* have a soul, don't you?

Stop running with Carolyn! Get back here!

There must be a hundred-fifty-two colors
in the squares and multiple lines. Stop fear.
That's what the patterns do. Stop dolor.
"I read that bright colors brighten you up,"
you said to your friend when you lived alone.
Then I appeared. Now I'm living alone.
Mauvelous, bluetiful, tickle-me-pink,
atomic tangerine, electric lime.
I'm tan, I'm *timberwolf*—you ran out of time.
I whiff them all; I take you up in sock-stink.

8.

I whiff them all. I take you up in sock-stink.
Could I archive thirty-eight pairs of socks?
In arranging them I find a way to think
unmellow yellow, brick red, shocking pink,
sunglow and *screamin green.* Feelings unlock
beyond simple rage or loss because nothing's
pure: *purple pizzazz, razzmatazz,* unblock.
No, I cannot archive running socks,
so photograph them next to books. Let go.
Return the good ones to the Ziploc bag
to take to Value Village—bright pairs show
me a way to live unmated. Something's
breaking up—is it my crying jag?
The widow's crayon box has legs.

9.

The widow's crayon box has legs, but
walking away isn't like running away.
Walking gives you time to feel your gut.
It actually gives you a chance to stay,
since you're going to have to anyway.
Alone, alone, alone, alive, alone
exploring the languishing emotions:
decay, then decline, *sepia*, then *silver.*
Isolated, edgy, weary restless gloom
worn with an *antique brass* lethargic gleam.
Bored, listless *chestnut*-colored apprehension,
the *charcoal* nothing-think of outer space
where lovethoughts go as I keep earthly pace.

10.

Lovethoughts go, and I keep earthly pace
while you run in Connecticut with Carolyn.
I'm shocked at how absent you are from our place,
our suite, our balcony, our marriage inn.
It's my condo bower now. I wander out
to the balcony garden where, below,
the post-Covid traffic's powering back.
Up here, striped bumblebees fly off. The screen door's open.
Why bother to close it? Hardly any other insects now.
No cats. No you to shout, *The screen door's open!*
The Great Extinction purples on. Without.
But a lone housefly zooms behind my back,
and I forgo my shower—can't coax a spider out.
Six legs. Eight legs. And wings (like you?). An insect world
wakes up inside. Outside: salvia buds unfurl.

11.

Wake up! Salvia's buds, like labia, unfurl.
Might as well masturbate—the widow's sex.
No one to interrupt. "Can I help you out?"
you'd say. *Jazzberry jam.* Why not fling my legs
across your side of the bed? Grip sheets. Uncurl.
In the last years of cancer sex I'd shout out,
"Honey, we did it!" To manage at last.
Tropical rainforest triumph. But thoughts,
ideas, notions, even evanescent
emotions, with tensile ephemeral strength
—*goldenrod, asparagus*—prove to outlast
the palpable, the muscle-like scent
that evaporates, then evokes. The length
of ideas? Infinity's stride. Translucent.
                              A naught.

12.

Now you're infinite. Translucent. You're naught.
Your quality of mind used to give a tint
of color to its transparency, so
I could just make out your lines of thought,
tracing their complexities—like water
lends air its aquamarine lucidity.
Thank you for sheer thinking. How I hope you
are thinking still as sudden structures of thought,
like architectural plans, blueprints-
in-air, materialize. Suddenly lines
that organize an enterprise—a novel,
say—come not sharply, but naturally clear,
like the sudden division, from our balcony,
of a sun shower, where a line of rain
appears in the sky, right there, marking the border
of a cloud too high to be seen.

13.

I'm under a cloud too high to be seen
by others. The widow cloud—so siriusly high
it casts the palest, the smallest, the greenest
blue-gray-violet shadowlet on me wherever I
walk, limp, stroll, even to the bakery
where I burst into tears over a . . .
    . . . a chocolate cupcake with sprinkles.

You had the palate of a little boy
and the carbohydrate capacity
to absorb an inch-thick layer of cocoa
with *piggy pink* and *laser lemon* dimples.
In this glass case I know which chocolate toy
you'd choose. I knew you. And I continue
to . . .
    That's the shadowlet:
                    it's knowing.
                            (It's you.)

14.

The shadowlet is knowing you without
the you you were. The knowing itself is
the palest scrim through which I see the world.
It doesn't dim the world—it just renames
all the tones, hues, values, but slightly—no doubt
that the colors are what they were—the *is*
of recognition of what was is whorled
inside each perception . . . Online I learned
"retired" colors get new Crayola names.
Maize departed, and *magic mint, teal blue* and
mulberry. Burnt sienna was saved. *Blue gray*
went. And *raw umber.* The widow's colors
got "retired." Well, I'm their living dolor, darling.
"Raw" and "magic" behind the scrim. Her and ~~him~~.

15.

Don't be X'ed out! Run! Run with Carolyn
in Connecticut. You can be everywhere now.
A new thought could come to me tomorrow
and my brain will wonder if *you* put it in.
(A little sexy, no? a post–sexual
mental insertion. A *mulberry* exertion.)
It's always summer where you are running.
There's an *always* because you are gone
like "blizzard blue" and five hundred
other color names. Who needs a séance?
Just live in the Retired Crayons Residence
with "goldfish gold" instead of *apricot*.
Carnelian? Is that the name for the shade
of forty–thousand–year–old handprints in a cave?

16.

Night yields to the turquoise sea, becoming young.
Don't be sorry if you cannot cry
in memory water. Just swim in it, I say.
Let's drop our sorrow-towels and dive—
you've vaporized, but your ideas are alive!
You're in your Asics, becoming myth.
I whiff you—unexpected sock-stink
mixed with waxy crayon box perfume.
Lovethoughts go; you keep a distant pace
beyond where labia unfurl like salvia.
Infinity's juggernaut—translucent?
Or just a cloud too high to be seen so far
above carnelian handprints in a cave
raw magic below the cloud's scrim (her/~~him~~)
casting a shadowlet of knowing
across a window: still, gray and mauve. Morning.

PART TWO

Before

THRESHOLD

We'd unhitched the shutters the night before
and went to sleep on the pallets we'd pushed
together to make a prenuptial bed,
the window framing a darkness we ignored
(too exhausted to make love), heads crushed
into skimpy pillows. We had fled
the first forty-five years of our lives for
this Spartan room, no surface lush
with objects, just a table and a lamp,
bags on the chair, suit and dress on the door.
I woke before you, a twenty-eight-year
habit after that. Here was the start: Lake,
opaline. Mountains, amethyst. To think
that window had been blank the night before!
And I didn't have to make the scene up: water,
sapphire; peaks, quartz. It wasn't art,
but a threshold—and we'd arrived there.

HELLO, LOVEBIRDS!

"Hello, lovebirds!" The newbie nurse
says to us, entwined in a hospital bed
(our island rectangle on a gray floor sea)
in this Covid Era in the cancer center,
on a limited four-hour visit that still
is boring (because there's nothing extra,
not even a plant in the room),
so we're streaming an Irish love story.
On the island of the screen, the soft-faced
actors-in-love talk at agonizingly
cross purposes—oh we know how that felt.
We broke up at that age, too.

"I'm going to interfere with your manliness,"
the nurse says, raising a navy-blue
plastic razor, like a miniature oar.
She needs to shave a patch of chest hair,
gray, but curly as seaweed,
so the heart monitor pads will stick.
Stymied, she leaves to get scissors
as scenes of Trinity College Dublin fly by.
We recognize it from all our visits
after we collided again as grownups.

"I haven't done this before," our nurse returns,
clips the seaweed patch on the beach of chest,
and dips the blue-oar razor in a paper cup of water.
We are fine today, by the way—he's not in pain.
Decades unroll behind us like seafoam—
what happened to Anxiety and Fear?
(Evaporated into the atmosphere . . .)
Using a tiny navy-blue oar to lift seaweed hair?
Pitifully ineffective. "We've got some shaving cream,"
I say. (We came equipped, of course.)

The green-blue gel foams up, the hair parts,
the sticky heart patch attaches to his skin,
and we all congratulate ourselves as she wafts out.
On the iPad, each actor lies in bed alone
with a tiny bright rectangle of a cell phone.
(You and I broke up from dorm rooms standing
at heavy, short-corded turtle-shaped receivers
with rotary dials like tillers, twelve recurrences ago.
Our cordless phone call came later, after
our paper letters had found one another.)
From his twin bed in Dublin, the young man
grabs his cell.
                    She has texted him.

TINKERBELL & MY HUSBAND

Of all the times I wished you would die quick,
my despair ballooning like a cartoon
bubble (but kept inside my face—tamped down
so you wouldn't notice), the worst
was when you'd sit in your chair reading,
glasses sliding down your nose. I cursed you then,
you looked so ordinary! Feeding your mind
with print, the light dimming around a sick
man in a velvet chair with a book, legs
crossed. My mind would snap to stage lights dimming
on the first play I ever saw: the time it took,
the ex-x-cruciating time in the too-big velvet seat
it took to see, through the dead dark quiet of all
the children, the tiny flicker of the spotlight
that was supposed to be Tinkerbell
dying.

   An adult voice came over telling us all
to shout, "LIVE!" and we did, and Tinker flickered,
so the voice said, "LOUDER." We yelled: she came alive.
But she was just a light standing in for a little being,
as tiny in all the universe as you were in your chair,
under a reading lamp, the circle of light closing
on the glare of current events—wasting
in the modern way of velvety agony.
I almost heard myself say, "LOUDER."

When the matinee was all over, the actors
assembled in a garish beam
(the house lights were up), all the characters
except Tinker. Tinkerbell wasn't there,
even though we'd yelled, "LIVE!"
She wasn't acted. She was electricity—
a current a stagehand had turned off.

THE LIFT

Reach. Touch. Button. Whoosh. Always let a child
press the elevator light. Up! Or down—
avoid doing it yourself, even if
the kid's a complete stranger. Slide. The mild
glide, sometimes the scrape, like a steel frown,
of the mammoth doors opening. Power
of one tiny digit (a parent has lifted
the little one to the arrow). Flicker of
accomplishment. That's what my husband wants.
From his wheelchair he has reached and lifted
his index finger. Look. Stretch. Strain. Quicker,
as I push him toward the button a stranger wants
to press first. But we get there! He lights the disc.
The metal coat opens to whisk us in.

THE PLEXIGLAS WALL

After our Plexiglas wall slams down: Rain.
Brainrain. Thinking feels like camping out.
At least I grabbed matches and plastic sheets
to pad the wet sod where I'll pitch our tent.
How far are we from our digital stove?
Just a few feet away from the wall this time:
I see right into our kitchen from this wilderness
where nothing makes sense but the urge to lift
the lid on my brainpan and plunge my hands
into the gray juicy curds—got to think
for both of us now! Over there, the laptop glows
on our granite counter, and the dishwasher
sloshes till the red "SANITIZED" is lit.
But out here I throw slop beneath the pines

as you lie on your camp cot, usurped by
bacteria—more drug trial side effects.
Fix lid back on skull. Make us a fire. Strike
match after match. My brain breathes and seeks
its secret child maneuver: Divide! Go
back through the wall, then type, syncopating
with microwave beeps, messages with plans
in thrall to a future, brief, quick, forbidden
as love letters—all the while keeping one

eye on you trying to sleep as the rain turns
to freezing pellets. So I grab my guilt,
zap it into a quilt, find the spot to slip
back through the glass, then tuck it on your cot:
a blanket for a shivering man in the wild.

PETTING MY HUSBAND'S
HEAD IN MY LAP

When I am so ill, I hope I can be
as soft as you are. This morning you turned
and looked back the way the cat,
climbing into the clothes hamper, stared at me
when he slowly inched in to recover.
As you've always explained, you are part cat.
You won't let me shave the back of your neck
or clean you up presentably human
because you need your fur. What I've learned
is not to push. You're another species.
Who *are* you? I've even shouted aloud,
hoping somehow you would say, "The same."
How thrilled I've been the times you called my name,
but you call it out as to a different mammal,
a human click-clucking to a tabby whose eyes
say, *who are you?* You taught me to meow. Me? Ow.
I careened into being your wife
like a cat shooting through all eight wheels
of a moving tractor trailer. Now it's you lighting off
across the street to begin your tenth life.

NOTES FROM SICK ROOMS

1.

*I have often wondered why it is considered a proof of virtue
in anyone to become a nurse.*
—Julia Prinsep Stephen, *Notes from Sick Rooms,* 1883

Who really wants to be a caregiver?
A kindness for the sick, a calling for
home-nursing the way Virginia Woolf's mother
described it—I could not tumble further
down into that self-free place. That was where
she found herself—as she slipped in behind
the fretfulness and want and fear of their
faces in need. She saw who she was there.
But I hated giving what I barely had away.
Losing myself in the tunnel of need,
down the gravityless jumble of trays,
cups, pills, towels . . . Then listening: to heed
the little voice, the yelp, the moan, the diminished
sound of the sick's claim. Because I was unfinished,
I faked it with efficiency.

2.

Faking it with efficiency came early,
the young self diverted into crisp plans.
A girl of twelve, cooking for her family
(giving recipes to her mother's friends!)
President of the sixth grade, all A's
except for math and gym. Which child is cold?
The efficient one. My parents' haze . . .
their dreams almost dreamed . . . their hopes' fractured mold
unable to make more hope, made me seek
a perfect outside, organized, promises met.
I'm not a baby! (Though I was.) *Or weak.*
(Who isn't weak? The sick are.) *You can bet
on me to come through!* My sturdy outside
like a stout cup, a thick glass, empty inside.

3.

Like a stout cup, a thick glass, empty inside,
the warm brew of mistakes and apologies
that makes a being human I decided
could never belong in me—what would fill
me was vigilance, always having to
be ready for emergencies.
Happily occupied and unaware . . . well,
that's a childhood where they say *I love you.*
Both you and I said that as kids.
Caregiving wasn't part of us. We just *were.*
Then we grew up and lost each other. When
I found you again, you'd been sick. Future: blur—
I imagined pushing your wheelchair. Back then
I didn't realize I was the invalid.

4.

There is, let us confess it (and illness is the great
confessional), a childish outspokenness in illness; things are
said, truths blurted out . . .

—Virginia Woolf, *On Being Ill*, 1930

How could I know I was an invalid?
That growing up too soon invalidated
childhood? Maturing falsely lifts the lid
of adulthood so fast. Childhood isn't shed.
It's looked for again and again. When it's found
as I found you—you were thirteen when I
saw you bouncing your leg beneath a desk
in the classroom across the hall, my des-
tiny darling—then childhood doesn't die.
Pandora's box? A toy box. (True growth refound.)
Along with lifting that secret door
to find a world fresh as a robin's egg
came illness—appearing at love's first stage.
I'm surprised I don't hate you more.

5.

I'm surprised I didn't hate my sister more.
Born ill, a preemie after the War,
she lay in a glass-topped incubator
while our mother lay still, at home in bed.
How good I was at playing quietly
(isn't poetry playing quietly?)
by her side or at the foot of her sickbed.
At her door, with beef broth, appeared Grandmother.
Julia Prinsep Stephen applauds beef tea.
I was never closer to my mother
than playing there, age three, with us three,
before a squalling sick infant was slipped
beneath our skin like a pox to inoculate
against pure love. Now love and illness mixed.

6.

Pure love, pure feeling, not love and illness mixed,
is like pure taste—the way kids won't mix
foods on their plates, each flavor separated.
(Too bad grownup plates aren't divided.)
With the purity of ginger chopped and brewed
I hated my sister. Such hatred cleared
the nostrils! My hatred of *you* combined
the salt-cinnamon of fury with thyme spines
of fear, the bay leaf of wariness,
and at 7pm I'd love-hate you most,
the exact time I had to deliver
dinner on your drug trial—timing those roast
fucking parsnips . . . that was the love-cleaver.
A caregiver really is a mother.

7.

It may seem difficult to follow this advice, but it is not.
Cheerfulness is a habit . . .
   —Julia Prinsep Stephen, *Notes from Sick Rooms,* 1883

A caregiver really is a mother.
How exhausting it is to mix the roles up.
Couldn't I ever just be a lover?
That's like longing for a plate divided up . . .
"If an invalid has to be fed, the meat
must be cut up most carefully, the patient's
tastes being scrupulously observed." Meet
Julia Prinsep Stephen, Queen of Patience.
I just can't separate my contempt from
my admiration—why admire a woman
who didn't think women should vote? Devote.
Her devotion made imaginary moats
like the ridges on a child's ceramic plate.
Love was love and hate was hate.

8.

Love was love and hate was hatred for crumbs.
Julia's "evil existence" of the "torrent of crumbs"
ignored by "the scientific world" is,
for caregiver and patient, on a par
with itches, bites, hangnails and slivers, points
of irritants that funnel the focus
so the plains of illness tornado to a point.
Yet it is simply a matter of sheets
to be swept, puffed and turned—Julia repeats
a caregiver's wet hands will calm the fuss
the patient makes by running damp fingers
into the crevasses till every crumb is gone.
Ok now? Excitement becomes a green lawn.
But a universe of ~~knots~~ "nots" lingers.

9.

Crumbs are little *nots*—not able, not well,
not happy, not calm, not a future, not a present
except what's not and what is, make a fretful
sweaty mess neatly divided into a seven-day pillbox.
Yes, it is division that will save the days.
This I have learned from my husband:
that moment by moment attention to the clock
of medication frees you into living as a diversion.
A pleasure is released from each
plastic click of a pillbox compartment, and green
and water and fur and breeze and
verandahs and bare feet on mown grass,
each soft spike prickly, not like a crumb,
but the gentle stimulation of nerve endings
that, in their waking, mean going on.

10.

If waking means going on, caretaking
really is a matter of efficiency.
Doing tasks leaves imagination free—
you have your day. "It" doesn't need faking,
for "it" is death, and caregiving is
one's consciousness of Huge. Love locates in
the hours one has, if crumbs don't interfere
to pretend that Huge is not there.
(If you'd like to make death a mere crumb,
just try to lie in bed with one.)
When a tiny bit becomes the universe,
it crowds you out. Yet you have a choice:
I must have understood this as a child
constructing a universe of wild and mild.

11.

*Considering how common illness is, how tremendous the
spiritual change that it brings, . . . what precipices and lawns
sprinkled with spring flowers a little rise of temperature
reveals . . .*

—Virginia Woolf, *On Being Ill*, 1930

Constructing a universe of wild from mild
involves selection—and arrangement is control.
How do I hate thee when I do? You child!
(Is that me or you?) I hate you till I call
out to that woman crossing the lawn,
the one who is an *I*, who isn't gone,
just out there for you, but not devoted.
Why don't you call her back to our bed?
Or call her to a rectangle on the lawn
and join her in a sport you played as kids—
oh let's be bad and play badminton
and let a shuttlecock fly until it dawns
on us that playing within white lines is fun,
a secret us-ness mapped within a grid.

12.

A secret us-ness mapped within a grid
for old-time battledore and shuttlecock—
let's leave this battle. Hey, shuttle your cock
over here! It's not all sickness all the time, kid . . .

And when I leave you to get on a plane
and hear the flight attendant instruct us
to put our own oxygen masks on first,
I'm grateful a whole industry thinks as I do.
It lets me withstand the shocked, dirty looks
from oncology nurses who feel I should be
at the hospital every minute, waiting
as I waited for my father in the car
to have his last drink at the bar and take
me home.
        Let me come and take you home.

13.

Let me come and take you home. Anger
covers terror, doesn't it? Whose terror?
Yours in the isolation room? Or mine
as I gown up to see you? It's an error!
Now, you're out. But all the tests don't get nearer
to an answer. You get better—if weaker,
your face like a sand painting shifting color,
not a stable, solid face, but one that signs
not-knowing, not-understood. You stood
your full height when they admitted you and
now, without a walker, you can't stand,
so you inch your way into the car.
After twenty-five years of this I don't say
I can't stand it anymore. Human beings
adjust to anything. Love stands up to fear.

14.

Love withstands fear and even hate
evaporates. In three weeks you gave up
the walker. In eight weeks we won at doubles.
In twelve weeks the body breakdown troubles
from the drug trial gone awry seem a mirage.
I'd rather be your doubles partner than sign up
for another illness stint. Is there Stage
Four Caregiver PTSD? I have it, mate!
Honey, I grieve. And owe more to Virginia,
who knew that we make do without sympathy,
than to her mother. "It is not easy," said Julia,
"even with the best intentions, for a nurse
to remain perfectly calm." Hey, it's not too late
for hysterical sex! Childhood re-seized. A universe
of verse—if averse, if things get worse.

15.

The art of being ill is no easy one to learn, but it is practiced to perfection by many of the greatest sufferers. The greatest sufferer is by no means the worst patient, and to give relief, even if it be only temporary, to such patients is perhaps a greater pleasure than can be found in the performance of any other duty.
— Julia Prinsep Stephen, *Notes from Sick Rooms,* 1883

Once I faked it with efficiency,
like a stout cup, a thick glass, empty inside,
and never realized I was an invalid
surprising myself by hating you so much.
(Pure love I wanted, not love and illness mixed!)
A caregiver's really a mother.
No! My wife's hate was the love-hate
that makes a universe of *I will nots.*
Yet I found un-knotting meant going on
to construct that universe from mild with wild,
a secret us-ness mapped within a grid.
Let me make you a home, my greatest sufferer.
We've adjusted to everything! Love stood up to fear.
If things get worse, I'll grieve, write verse, make
giving you relief my pleasure in reverse: home nurse.

IN THE MOOD

Post drug trial; Covid

Once it was clear that we could die,
we thought, Let's make the end sweet.
Zip it. No whining. Each day repeat
the smile of routine. Don't lie.
Living in nine hundred sixty square feet:
get out the exercise sheet.
Noon: yoga; 3pm: squats and weights.
After the dinner we cook together
(squash lasagna) exquisite, since we make
it step-by-step (no email on the side),
we limit the news, read, then have our triumph:
blasting "In the Mood" as we step-glide
two thousand steps round our suite.
                            Our omph-
alos: the bed! We reach for one another,
if only verbally (we've both been
murmuring a steady commentary
on all we've pondered through the day—
except the thought that both of us could die).
If we can choose our end, we choose it this way.

TINY THINGS

Inside conflagrations
tiny things:
a "t" flies off a word;
a protestor re-snaps
the flap on her bag that
never really keeps snapped
as she lugs her sign;
a semicolon tries to take
the place of an "and";
(you; me?)
the slightly overstretched
elastic on a mask
falls off an ear;
an itchy long-ago remark
hardens into a pea-stone
under mattress-layers
of the unconscious
(ok, princess . . .).
See that dot?
That's what's left
after a brain tumor's
radiated.

All the tiny things
diverting from
the big thing:
THE ISSUE
(you're dying).
Or is that tissue?
The flying "t"
just landed like a cormorant
at the end of a dock
changing the view.
(I blow my nose.)
Don't fly away!
I promise I'll stop crying
and let go of
hardened things.
The bird stays,
wings outstretched
in a mind-inlet,
and I see a different way.
But a bra strap doesn't stay:
in the bottom corner of
a video the protestor
subtly hikes hers up again.

A world hangs on a hangnail.
As a semicolon rises
and flies off, leaving
the shape of an ear
upside down in the air,
your life turns at the touch
of a radiologist's pinky
till your tumor's a mere pea-stone
(ok, prince . . .).
THE ISSUE is
driven into a dot,
and I knot the elastic
of our masks to keep them on
while you're transferred
to a gurney, just as
an ampersand
sneaks back,
joining you & me.
Hug that logogram!
It isn't the end
of the sentence yet

A TINY MENTAL FLASH ON A RED FOOTSTOOL

Perched on the edge of a red wool footstool,
spine just comfortably meeting a hard spot
beneath the tapestry, I'm connected
to the thing made. My desperately ill mate
joylessly says, *Don't sit like that.* Like what?
Supported by a red woven center?
My energized posture has grown to annoy him.
Caregiving comes to this. (You can't sit
as you like; you must get up, and do, with
resentment sometimes so cold it's another spine
supporting your spine.) As I rise, I see
every boyfriend from my whole life, their faces
in tender, liquid sympathy, looking up at me,
in their eyes the same mute shock I feel, but
the guys say nothing as I stand up and reach—

SEX AFTER SEVENTY

After we cleaned out our closets
we started on our sex lives.
No new techniques—just forgiving debts.
After we cleaned out one closet
we discovered another room back there:

                          & met
as a long surprise of a spring afternoon arrived
through the threshold of that closet
on a spare bed we'd been saving all our lives.

ROUTINES

Routines are destiny.
Making it up as you go along
wastes the fireworks energy.
Routines are destiny,
a blanket below the night sky.
Lie down on routines. Look up. See?
A pyrotechnic possibility.
Routines are destiny—
when you make it up, you stumble along.

PANCAKE ODE

Buckwheat disc with a crispy edge,
stave off mourning, morning flirt.
Little pancake like a ledge
(stave off mourning, morning flirt)
from which to peer out at the world,
two-dimensional globe unfurled.
Fat raspberries and thick yogurt,
what makes you so alive to eat?
Nutmeg, baking soda, salt.
What makes me so alive I eat
a buckwheat disc with a crispy edge?
Now I walk out on a ledge
(nutmeg, baking soda, salt)
to greet the last days of chez nous.
I love you. I'm sorry. What will we do?

WHERE DOES IT LIVE?

Where does it live?
you would ask me.
Saucer, cup, spoon—
which shelf, which drawer.
"You might not come home . . ."
I know, you said.
Three paramedics
had just burst in.

Everything had
to have its spot:
book, shirt, key, shoe.
Where does it live?
pen, tape, plug, file.
They picked you up.
Nail, wrench, hammer, awl.
They carried you out.

I grabbed my coat.
For a moment
an unhinged storm:
knives leapt from drawers,
extension cords,
pliers, screwdrivers
from cabinet doors:
bowls, pots, towels,
paperclips, Band-Aids . . .

Where do we live?
Where do we live?
As plastic containers flew,
I slammed the door
and ran toward you.
Where do you live?

And after a long
time, I returned.
Like excited pets
who'd finally settled,
they'd slipped back
to their shelves and slept
for their doors were shut
when I entered alone.

PART THREE

When

DECIDING TO END YOUR LIFE, YOU THANK ME

MAID: Medical Assistance in Dying, Toronto

When you looked up and said, "Thank you," I saw
your gratitude rise over us like rain.
It seemed external to us both—an awe
of what we were about to do (a sane
alternative to modern agony).
The dryness between us had been like climate,
like desiccation, like chapped lips only
chapped *everything*. You'd stopped being a mate,
stopped thanking. I'd begun drying up rough
as a towel in wind.
                So, your thank you *was* rain.
It swept through like a front—one thanks enough
to drench everything. It was pouring! Plain
moisture plumping cells from without—and within . . .
I stood getting soaked to a rapid bloom,
knowing you knew the wasteland we'd been in,
and, from this, we'd make your desert garden.

MY NEXT HUSBAND IS SOLITUDE

"Your next husband," you muttered,
facing out the window from your last bed.
To your back I whispered, "No, no, no next,"
with a gruff animal hoarseness
that shocked me because it wasn't uttered
in response but defying what you said.

I was refusing the thought of any "next."
To tender myself to the honeyed forcedness
of future love-soothe for someone else?
More work of being a syrup balm would kill me!
"No, no, no next" meant I'd die, too.

After you I want a lapping blue calm,
to act, not as a woman, but a pond,
a lonely enigma in others' eyes,
but in my own eyes, pooled, satisfied.

What if you let solitude be next for me,
your ghost on a bench overlooking
my blue austerity?

THE NEXT WORLD IS ONE OF IDEAS

MAID: Medical Assistance in Dying, Toronto

About his death, we
Talked without words, then came time
For the INTERVIEWS

Loss of hearing not
Quite total for either the old
Doctor—or my husband

(She held a tiny
Amplifier)—so they yelled
Whole floor knew his wish:

Medical Assistance
In Dying Three witnesses
List Pen Loop-signed X'ed

A second doctor came
In blue metallic glasses:
The INTERVENTION

I've held cats for this
Now him, soft favorite shirt
When he heard "in fifteen

Minutes" he sank
Went still as snow—no thrash
No rattle, just the glide

The long, furred body
I loved even to his death
My head on his chest

Warm earth   I shifted
Not to hear his stopped heart
The clock   his last view

Held his hand until
It cooled to a waxy gray
The suitcase waiting

The next world is one
Of ideas—
                    are those his?
Glass shapes in the sun!

His clear thoughts refract
All their angles made known

Have you received thoughts
And wondered why they've not
Occurred to you before?

They could be his

CREMATION ROOM:
Invited to Press the Button

Conveyor belt ov–
er trap door in the floor:
your coffin rises

it's the box of you
lightly bumped onto the belt
I know it *is* you

mind and spirit flown
because I saw the white cloth
your nose and your cheeks

START button awaits
a big pearl on a column
two steps away: I press

room so cold, clean, and beige
my coat is on   you are gone
and also going

the belt is moving
huge steel doors flush with the wall
open to the heat

my face feels the fire
eyes suddenly see inside
the brick chimney charred

scorched from scores of years
the color of horses' hooves
and you go   go IN

not into a blast
but a glow from a blaze below
its source I can't see

steel doors sliding like
drapery in this room so cold
I can see my breath

PART FOUR

Afterglow

Afterglow

THE AFTERGLOW

I miss our wordlessness
The brief touch of the hand
Like a whisper, midback

Now I live in the afterglow
Purple and peach streaks
Behind the near-night clouds

But getting used to twilight
Reaching out for the back of a chair
To guide me . . . I still can see . . .

With your hand on my back
A big decision could get made
A big move

And all without words
As wordlessly
You would come into me

And I got up afterwards
You lying there alone
I stumbling out alone

THE CALM

About a blanket being held open
A hand on the hemstitch of that flap

About this feeling I will never feel again
About this feeling you never felt since

You held the blanket, your arm, the whiff
Of your armpit, the flesh of you who

Never wore clothes in bed, your nakedness
Felt all the way through my travel clothes

My purse and my suitcase dropped in the hall
And all the rushing, checkpoints, and rain

Flying into the night like pinpoint lights
Blinking off, off, off, a calmness closing

A calm I can never induce in myself
Only you could do it, no one else even

My mother (I was too tiny then
To feel the need for adult calm though

I yearn for it now as a child yearns)
Years of adulthood's anxious doing and

Fixing and shouldering and talk-managing
Flung me so far away from myself

That I spun in an orbit of Outerness
A galaxy forlorn

So felt as that blanket flap opened
The mothering of a lover returning

A lost childhood to his beloved and
Down, down, down to a deep-sea calm, plumbed

Home   Hall   Bed   In

To do this for myself now that you are gone eternally
Is so impossible

That my only recourse is to make it unnecessary
(Not that you, now burnt to ashes, are unnecessary)

But since I cannot provide for myself the shift
From Lost Without to Found Within,

I must stay . . . somewhat . . . calm,
And, as if on a blanket on sand, lie alone

Somewhat naked.

ORGANIC SADNESS, COMPOST STYLE

Instead of beating or pulsing inside
Instead of lubdub, the heat inside

Of things breaking down—it's rich, it's loam
Of people decomposing into loam

Of the people you've collected over years
Of those who've lived inside you over years

All in a melting, merging, mushing heap
All in a flecked brown compost heap

Like music shredding, no shedding, its notes
Like light loosing, no losing, its motes

Like a lush everything into every other thing
Like a paste of waste of every into thing

All they all meant becoming feeling
All umber inside the umbra of feeling

MOVED & TOUCHED

If loneliness spreads like an abscess,
does that mean I don't want to live anymore?
Not at all. Even poisoned by absence
I am so curious about my own
ill state that I watch my bruised life and know why
purple is the color of the mourning eye.
It's the hue of distance that people wear,
richly dark, the best color for velvet. Smoothed
in one direction, velvet's nap is like a nap,
restorative. But the other direction
is revelatory, the roots of threads. That soothes,
too. Understanding the fabric of absence,
the soft, thready scent of lost affection,
is what gives loneliness its worth.
It *is* worth living in this state: a cloth map!
You're my velvet guide, my rest of life by touch.
When I feel moved and then say I am touched,
an absence inside me is suddenly tapped.

QUESTION

Is the soul hairless?
Does it never secrete or flake?

Does it not have bunions?
As the soul ages, doesn't it have days

when it's difficult to walk?
Scratching and sneezing,

won't it forget
its guest?

Elbow and spine,
pancreas and liver,

hysterias and amusements,
have I behaved myself?

Have I,
    . . . overstayed?

I'll have to let
Soul be the judge of that,

its bald head gleaming,
or, if Soul is a lily,

simply nodding in the gusts,
or, if it's wind,

simply breezing
its caress

on the bare leg
of its guest.

THE REALIZATION

How does the realization arrive?
I don't know—it was suddenly here.
I marked his death each month for most of a year.
At first the relief allowed me to thrive.
Then: I watched a purpled loneliness creep
up the days like a line of infection
from a poison bite up an arm. Then: a leap
and the realization (from every direction!)
thought-grabbed me—an attack from behind.
(It *wasn't* a sinister creeping line.)
It was EVERYWHERE:
                    I will die alone
in the hands of strangers.
                    No legal
document's tone, however regal, will
prevent it. My lifelong friend is gone.

TODAY MY TASK IS THE CODICIL

Contemplating life being over
in the panic weeks as the triage of the ill
sorts the ones like me to die . . . I must accept
being passed by: I've had my pomegranate life.
Seeds sluicing red . . . Rose affection.
Vermilion dread. The juice: friends of fifty years,
you in your sweatpants and virus mask . . .
Crisp gold type on a black, matte folder.
Like 81% of those over
the age of 72, I have one:
Will. Just one vowel away from being well,
as I am now. But today my task is the codicil
that designates the little stuff: a paperweight, a watercolor,
six leather volumes of Mrs. Delany's letters,
typed in a Docx to send to Wills and Trusts,
so a healthy stranger, young and un-
known to me now, will see to what she must.

MY LATE HUSBAND'S FILE STYLE:
Facing a Ceiling-Tall Five-Drawer Lateral File Cabinet

Dizzy! Staircases at every brain angle—
are they moving? Mental escalators
shudder between shifting thought-floors, angles
of organization never clear
to me. Cloudy! Your once-lucid design.
Could you have denied you were dying just
to insist I plunge then climb—no arrows, no signs—
through the interior of you at last?
Now that your warm organs, warm hands, warm limbs
are gone, it's your systems I live in:
cabinet-gray Escher-like optical illusions.
Will I ever find my way? Triple passwords . . .

The heart of you I'm working towards . . .
files within files.

Now you have admitted me!

As you couldn't admit you were dying to me.

LOVE LETTER IN THE STORAGE LOCKER

All the papers cram-dumped in boxes in haste
unstuffed, unpacked, uncrunched, unwedged this late

in life strikes the lover still.
                              Against one-rushed time,

the stillness opens up the past's chest,
rediscovery now recovery.

Dust puffs up. Moats materialize the old love.

Which one is realer? Then, when so much younger? No,
it's *now*, warm for a moment, in the arms of a folder.

FIOR DE ZUCCA

A memory bloomed
like a zucchini flower
I pan fried and ate.

THE YOU-SPOT

Our hands and feet were the same size, though you
were a little bit taller—the perfect fit!
I feel your hand on my back passing through
my vertebrae as if toward my heart—it fits
right there between my shoulder blades, my ghost.
It's the You-Spot. The place of consummate
sympathy you couldn't have as a human mate
who'd never intuit *all* my feelings—lost
in the married wilderness between us even
when your actual hand was at my real back—
because who can be expected to *be* all of that?

But now that you live in my mind we're more even
than even we were; your ghost hand's the sympathy
I yearned for but couldn't humanly have before.

THE FAWN

From a waking world, it's hard to go dreamside,
but that's how it was: where inside met
outside at once. I slept on a platform
of a three-walled house that opened to the woods.
(Fast asleep inside my sleep!) Morning.
I only felt the light. My eyes were closed.
And there was something else, raspy but soft,
moist against my cheek:

                the lapping tongue of a fawn.
The fawn had settled beside my bedclothes.
When I opened my eyes in this dream of waking
I could only have had when asleep, it was dawn.
The fawn's nose was black and wet, its tongue
a forest pink.

              It filled me with a speckled softness.
You'd been dead nine months.
My new life licked at me.
I was just as old as I am now in the dream,
but I had a child-thought as I stared
into the liquid eyes of the deer: *it's talking
just to me,* not in words, but in understanding.
Neither the deer nor I were yet standing.

WIDOW IN KITCHEN WITH YELLOW APPLE

You burst through the door
wheeling your red Swiss
Army suitcase—how had
you packed all you needed
in that for ten months?
—and I, in my stained yoga pants
stood gaping with delight
(my little red paring knife
in one hand and a yellow
apple in the other).
You're home! I smiled,
my face stretching so wide
I'd forgotten skin
could be so elastic,
and as you bumbled
with your suitcase (had
you brought me a present?
your beard needed a trim . . .)
you looked up and said,
Yellow? I only buy
yellow apples now
I almost said but
instead chirped, *It's time*
for the new crop of
Honey Crisps! Red, round.
I'll buy you some red ones,

I said, looking in
your pain-free face, tired
from a journey but
exhilarated to be
home—eyes bright green
—we hadn't even kissed yet.
It was Saturday,
and I had to stick
my hair in a band and
grab my jacket or there
would be nothing left
at the farmer's market,
so I almost stumbled
into you in my rush
to supply your wants,
slightly turning my ankle
against the wheel of
your red Swiss Army
suitcase disappearing
against the door so
securely locked: big
white rectangle shut.
You'd been so real each
hair of your beard glistened
with the outside's cold air.
The hair on your knuckles

gripping the black handle
curled in little squiggles
as if drawn by a fine
line marker: I saw them,
saw them, the point
of my red paring knife
poised at the yellow peel,
you'd been so real.

HONEY CRISP

Hello wizenface, hello apple
understudy in the fridge
since March (it's September)
hello wrinkly red cheeks,
I'll bet you're almost a year old,
born last autumn
kept in the fruit storage built
half-underground on the farm
then, in the snow, sold to me.
Hello my honey crisp (well,
my honey, no longer crisp . . .)
are you asking why you
haven't been eaten by now?

Because that man hewed to his routines:
an apple for lunch every day
the same red punctuation.
You were earmarked for the date
he slipped from my arms & we both
slid to the floor, red angel, are you
listening? 911, hospital, hospice
and ten days later (you were
about six months old then)
he died and was carried
to a cold shelf.

Hello smiley-stem, hello days
moving you from spot to spot.
Hello week where I forgot
and left you at the back and
went about my new life.
Greetings new groceries!
Their jumble causes a re-
arrangement of your bin
so I have to pick you up
—would you rather
have been eaten and
lived on as energy?
Not yet, not yet, my pomme.
Hello soft wrinkled
face in my palms.

Notes

Note: The occasional cross-out and the lack of punctuation in certain poems is intentional.

"The Widow's Crayon Box": The color names in quotations or in italics are those of past or present Crayola crayons.

"Notes from Sick Rooms": the epigraphs from Julia Princep Stephen and from Virginia Woolf are excerpted from *On Being Ill, Introduction by Hermione Lee, with Notes from Sick Rooms by Julia Stephen*, Paris Press, 2012.

"Deciding to End Your Life, You Thank Me" and "The Next World Is One of Ideas": Medical Assistance in Dying, or MAID, is a process in Canada that allows a qualified candidate to receive assistance from a medical practitioner in ending the candidate's life. In the case referred to in the poem, a physician directly injected a lethal drug.

Notes

Acknowledgments

Grateful acknowledgment is made to the following journals and anthologies for publishing many of the poems in this book, often in earlier versions:

American Poetry Review: "Afterglow" and "Touched"

Donne and Contemporary Poetry: "The Plexiglas Wall"

Ecotone: "Pancake Ode"

Grain Anniversary Issue (Canada): "The Widow's Crayola Box" (excerpted from "The Widow's Crayon Box")

The Hudson Review: "The Shadowlet" and "The Widow's Cloud" are reprinted by permission of *The Hudson Review*, Volume LXXVII, No.1 (Spring 2024). (Excerpted from "The Widow's Crayon Box")

Juniper (Canada): "Fior de Zucca"

Liber: A Feminist Review: "In the Mood," "Petting My Husband's Head in My Lap," "Question," "The Calm," "Cremation Room," "The You-Spot," and "A Tiny Mental Flash on a Red Footstool"

The Orchards Poetry Journal: "Routines"

Poetry: "Deciding to End Your Life, You Thank Me," "Tinkerbell & My Husband," and "Widow in Kitchen with Yellow Apple"

Poetry East: "My Next Husband Is Solitude"

Plume: "Hello, Lovebirds," "The Next World Is One of Ideas," "Notes from Sick Rooms," "Threshold," and "Where Does It Live?"

Shenandoah: "Organic Sadness, Compost Style"

The Walrus (Canada): "Honey Crisp" and "Today My Task Is the Codicil"

With Thanks to:

My editor, Jill Bialosky, for her editorial acumen and kindnesses over many years; my agent, Alexa Stark, for her knowing support; Hollay Ghadery at *River Street* for her social media guidance; Laura Mucha, Nancy Palmquist, Sarahmay Wilkinson, Gwen Cullen, Dassi Zeidel, and Gina Savoy at W. W. Norton & Company for their production genius and general flare, as well as Elizabeth Scanlon at *American Poetry Review*, Anna Lena Phillips Bell at *Ecotone*, Paula Deitz at *The Hudson Review*, Katha Pollitt at *Liber*, Adrian Matejka and Holly Amos at *Poetry*, Daniel Lawless at *Plume*, Richard Jones at *Poetry East*, Lesley Wheeler at *Shenandoah*, as well as Jim Johnstone at *Grain*, Lisa Young at *Juniper*, and Carmine Starnino at *The Walrus*, for their stalwart support of my poems.

My friends inspire my poetry in unexpected ways. Thanks to Phillis Levin for her sympathetic eye over all the lines in this book, to Rachel Hadas for numerous conversations that affected these poems, to Carolyn Hill-Bjerke for memories of her encounters with my late husband, to James Cummins for his weekly enthusiasm, and to Richard Watson for his seriously playful focus on the body of my work.

Bio

Molly Peacock is the author of eight collections of poetry, including *The Analyst: Poems* and *Cornucopia: New and Selected Poems*. Her poems appear in leading literary journals and are anthologized in *The Oxford Book of American Poetry*. Former president of the Poetry Society of America and former poet-in-residence at the American Poets' Corner, she is the cofounder of *Poetry in Motion* on New York's subways and buses and the founder of *The Best Canadian Poetry*. Her latest project is *Molly Peacock's Secret Poetry Room*, a creative space for first-generation college students to write at Binghamton University. Recipient of fellowships from the Ingram Merrill Foundation, the New York Council on the Arts, the National Endowment for the Arts, the Canada Council on the Arts, Access Copyright Canada, the Society for Citizens and Scholars, and the Leon Levy Center for Biography, Peacock is also the author of two biographies about creativity in the lives of women artists: *The Paper Garden: Mrs. Delany Begins Her Life's Work at 72* and *Flower Diary: Mary Hiester Reid Paints, Travels, Marries & Opens a Door*. From a binational American and Canadian family, she lives in Toronto and teaches at 92NY in New York City.